Arabic For Beginners
"Arabic Reading and Writing"
Second Edition

Arabic For Beginners
"Arabic Reading and Writing"

Written by
Ali Almaleki

Voyage  Books

First Published in Britain by Mediaserve Productions 1984.
Revised edition published by Voyage Books (the Book division of Mediaserve Productions) 1986

Distributed by
VOYAGE BOOKS
4 Carlisle Street,
London W1V 5RG
Tel: 01 434 2941.

Copyright © Mediaserve Productions 1984, 1986 ISBN   0   947 930 02   7

Printed and bound in Britain by the Trade Printing Company

This book is sold subject to the condition that it shall not, by way of trade or otherwise, be lent, re-sold, hired out, or otherwise circulated without the publisher's prior consent in any form of binding or cover other than that in which it is published and without a similar condition including this condition being imposed on the subsequent purchaser.

This book is designed to help readers read and write Arabic through matching the sounds of some Arabic letters with the English ones or in other cases by physical description if there is no similarity.
Readers should notice the following points:—

1. *Arabic is written from right to left*

2. *Apart from school books all vowels (fat-ha, kassrah, damah) are written only in the Koran and other books; elsewhere they are used sparingly. We have used them in this book because they are a necessary part of Arabic and students can omit them when they have mastered Arabic reading and writing at a more advanced level then their initial elementary study.*

3. *A question mark, comma, and semicolon are written in Arabic as* ؟ ، ؛

We have tried to use simple words and sentences in order to simplify Arabic to our readers at this stage of study.

A. Al maleki

Chapter One

It is pronounced as "a" in far, and written	ا
	اَ اِ اُ
Like "d" in did	د
	دَ دِ دُ
Like "r" in rat	ر
	رَ رِ رُ

Pronounce the following syllables:

Like "da" in dart	دا
Like "ra" in rat	را

Read

Like "dar" in dart	دار

Chapter Two

Like "oo" in food or moon	و

و

Pronounce the following syllables:

Like do	دو

Like "wid" in widow	ود

Read

دور   دور   دار   دار

Chapter Three

Isolated Final	Linked Final	Medial	Initial
ن	ـن	ـنـ	نـ

This letter like "n" in nap

It is written

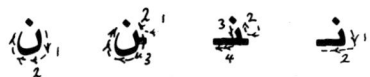

Pronounce the following syllables:

Like « na » in nasty	نا
Like "noo" in noon	نو
Like "win" in wind	
Like « ra » in rat	را

Read

نور   نار   داران   دور   دار

Chapter Four

Like "z" in zigzag ز

زِ زَ زُ

Pronounce the following syllables:

Like "za" in zigzag زا

Like zoo زو

Read

دار دور داران نار نور زاد زار

Vocabulary

a house	دار
houses	دور
two houses	داران
fire	نار
light	نور
cooked food	زاد
he visited	زار

Grammar:

Letters as

ر　و　ا　ز　د

might be linked to the preceding letters i.e.

نار نور

But never be linked to the following ones i.e.

زار زاد دور

Exercise 1

Make syllables from the following letters:

1) a. د   b. ا
2) a. ن   b. و
3) a. د   b. و
4) a. ن   b. ا
5) a. ا   b. ر

Exercise 2

make words from the following syllables and letters:

1) a. دا   b. ر
2) a. نا   b. ر
3) a. دا   b. را   c. ن
4) a. ن   b. و   c. ر

Chapter Five

L.F.	I.F.	Mc.	In.
ي	ي	ـيـ	يـ

Like "y' in yesterday

Pronounce the following syllables:

Like "ya" in yard	يا
Like "you"	يو
Like "we"	وي
Like "re" in read	ري
Like "nee" need	ني
Like "de" in detail	دي

Read:

دار   نوري ✪   داري   نوري   رازي ✪

زاراني   دينار   ديناران

✪ This sign means a name.

Chapter Six

ب‍ ب‍ ب ب

Like "b" in bat

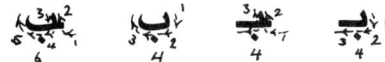

Pronounce the following syllables:

Like "ba" in bath	با
Like "bo" in bone	بو
Like "bee"	بي

Read

باب   دار   رازي   بابان   بابي

بیر   بوران

Vocabulary:

My house	داري
a door	باب
two doors	بابان
My door	بابي
a well	بير
a currency unit used in some Arab countries:— Iraq, Kuwait, **Libya**	دينار

Chapter Seven

It is called fat-ha and pronounced like "a" in make. This is a vowel and must be positioned above the letter concerned. i.e.

َ زْ زَ

Pronounce the following syllables:—

Like "ra" in rate رَ

Like "ye" in yellow يَ

Like "ne" in net نَ

Like "wea" in weather وَ

Read:

نُورِي زَازَ رَبَابْ بَرِيد ذَرب

Vocabulary:

Post (letters, parcels)   بَرید

Way   دَرب

Exercise 3

Form words from the following vowels and letters by placing fat-ha in proper place and choosing the right shape of letters:

1) a. ر   b. ـَـ   c. ب   d. ا   e. ب
2) a. ب   b. ـَـ   c. ر   d. ي   e. د
3) a. د   b. ـَـ   c. ر   d. ب
4) a. ب   b. ـَـ   c. د   d. ر

Chapter Eight

ـم م مـ م

Like "m" in made

Pronounce the following syllables

Like "ma" in man ما

Like "me" مي

Like "me" in men مَ

Read:

نامَ رَمزي   ما نامَ بَدرٌ

نَديمٌ يَزور مَردانٌ   مَنام بَدري   ميزان

Vocabulary

Slept	نام
He didn't sleep	ما نام
he visits	يَزور
scale	ميزان
bed	مَنام

Chapter Nine

ق ـق ـقـ قـ

This letter can not be described by any English letter but what we can say it is the furthest back "k" sound you can make, with the back of the tongue closing the arches of the back of the mouth.

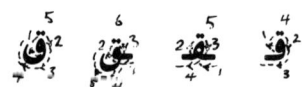

Read

قامَ   مَرزوق   يَنام قَدري   زَورَق نَديم

نَديم   قَمَر   قَريب

Vocabulary

He stood	قامَ
boat	زَورَق
moon	قَمَر
near	قَريب

Chapter Ten

ّ

This sign called "Shaddah" and used to strengthen the letter which is positioned above it to sound like double letters. Shaddah is written above the letter.

Pronounce the follwing syllables:

Like "woo" in wood   وّ

Like "dd" in add   دّ

If there is fat-ha above the same letter which has to have shaddah, shaddah is written below fat-ha i.e.

Like "wa" in wake   وَّ

Read

Vocabulary

he knocked   دَقَّ
god   رَبّ
prophet   نَبِيّ

Chapter Eleven

It is called Kesrah and pronounced like "i" in will and positioned below the letter some time is written under shaddah and above the letter i.e.

ـِ

رِّ

Pronounce the following syllables:

Like "wi" in wind وِ

Like « ri » in river رِ

Like "me" مِ

Read

مازِنْ قادِم
رامِزْ مَرَّ مِن دربِنا

Vocabulary

he is coming	قادِم
he passed	مَرَّ
from	مِن
way	دَرب

Chapter Twelve

It is called "damah" and positioned above the letter. **Damah** has to be pronounced lighter than the letter like "u" in duck

Pronounce the following syllables:

Like « do » in doctor: ذُ

Like "wro" in wrote رُ

Read

مُنيرْ ○ مُدير
مُراد ○ نامَ

Manager مُدير

Chapter Thirteen

Like "f" in fat

فَ فُ فِ

Pronounce the following syllables:

like "fa" in father	فا
Like "foo" in food	فو
Like "fee" in feed	في

Read

رَفّ
رَديف۰ في دارِ مُفيد۰
فاروق۰ فَنّان

Vocabulary

shelf	رَفّ
in	في
artist	فَنّان

Chapter Fourteen

ل   ـل   ـلـ   لـ

Like "L" in lap

لِ   لُ   لَ   لْ

Pronounce the follwing syllables:

Like "Le" in Let	لِ
Like "Lea" in Leaf	لِي
Like "La" in Ladder	لَا

Read

بِلَال ۞ لَا يَنَامُ فِي دَارِ رَازِي ۞

Vocabulary

no	لَا
he sleeps	يَنَام

Grammar

When there is «ا» following «ل» 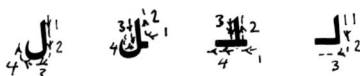 has to be written in the middle of " لـ " as لا their combination never be linked to the following letter as we mentioned above in بلال

Chapter Fifteen

"Hamzah"
It is written on several forms, and we prefer you to leave its details till you reach Chapter Thirty Nine.

Like "a" in ate أَ

أَب
أَرادَ نوري۠ أَن يَقرَأ

Like "a" in at ءِ

Read ماء ، نوري۠ بَنّاء

ء is mostly written above if there is a following letter which has to be linked with i.e.

فائِز۠ دائِم بِئر

Like "o" in oriental أُ

أُ

Read

أُم

أُريد أَن أَزورَ رازي

Like "i" in "inner"

إِ

إِ

Read

إِقرَأ . إِناء

Vocabulary:

father	أَب
he want	أَراد
to (but it doesn't mean as in I am going to London)	أَن
he reads	يَقرَأ
water	ماء
builder	بَنّاء
winner (m)	فائِز
permanent	دائِم
well	بِئر
mother	أُم
I want	أُريد
to visit	أَزور
read (demand)	إقرأ
dish	إناء

Chapter Sixteen

ط

As a kind of "t" made with tongue behind the upper teeth

Read

طابوق قِطار
طارِق طَبيب . لُطفي طالِب

Vocabulary:

bricks	طابوق
train	قِطار
doctor	طَبيب
student	طالِب

Chapter Seventeen

"Tenween"

It occurs only with nouns and adjectives and used without the definite article, and situated above or below the final letter

Like un ____ ٌ ____ ٍ ____

Like an ____ ً ____ ً ____

Like in ____ ٍ ____ ٍ ____

Read

لَبيبٌ واقِفٌ وَراءَ زَوْرَقٍ

وِدادٌ يَرمي وَرَقاً في نارٍ

Vocabulary:

he stands واقِف
behind وَراء

he throws يَرمي
paper وَرَق

Chapter Eighteen

"Hamzatulwasel" Liaison
hamzatulwasel never be voiced but it
serves our continuous reading

قَفَزَ اَلْوَلَدُ

We pronounce the above sentence as
"Kafazalualadu", so we moved
through our reading the sentence from
the first word to the second one
without stoppage.

Vocabulary:

he jumped قَفَزَ

boy وَلَد

** One way of making a noun
definite is to give it the definite article
al (ال) which is written in front of
the noun and joined to it, اَلْوَلَد
means the boy

Chapter Ninteen

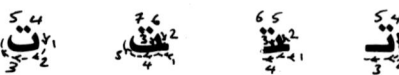

It is pronounced as "t" in tap

Pronounce the following syllables:

Like « te » in test	ت
Like "tr" in tree	تر
Like « ta » in task	تا
Like "tou" in tour	تو

Read

لَمياءُ تَقرَأُ ، بَتولُ نادَت رَمزي

أنتَ ما قَرَأتَ

* * This letter is called taa taweelah ت (long taa) to be distinguished from the Taa Kasserah (short taa), see Chapter Twenty Eight.

Vocabulary:

She reads	تَقرَأ
She call	نادَت
You	أَنت
You read	قَرَأت

Chapter Twenty

سـ ـسـ ـس س

Like "s" in sat (never as in was)

يَسْ يَسِّ يَسَّ يَسُّ

Pronounce the following syllables:

Like « se » in sell	سَ
Like « sa » in saturday	سا
Like "si" in sister	سِ
Like "see" in seed	سي

Read

سافَرَ سامي بالقِطار
مَيسون سَأَلَت فارِس
طَقسُ بارِد

Vocabulary:

he travelled	سافَر
by train	بالقِطار
she asked	سَألت
weather	طقس
cold	بارِد

Chapter Twenty One

The following letter resembles nothing in English, and it has to be voiced from the 'throat and larynx'' with tightened throat and squeezed larynx.

ع ـع ـعـ عـ

عِ عَـ جِـ عُـ

Read

عِمران طالِبٌ
سُعادُ تَلعَبُ مَعَ نَعيمٍ
عادَ سَعدونُ مِنَ العَمَلِ
مَناعٌ يُطيعُ المُعَلِّمَ

Vocabulary:

she plays	تَلعب
with	مع
he came back	عاد
work	عَمَل
he obeys	يُطيع
teacher	مُعَلِّم

Chapter Twenty Two

"Maddah"

When hamzah is followed by the letter
' ا ' both become "Maddah" آ

آ

Read

آباء
قَرَأَ وديعٌ ۞ اَلقرآن

Vocabulary :

fathers آباء

Koran قُرآن

Chapter Twenty Three

ى

Like "a" in far

يٓ

* * We learned « ا » but in some words "a" takes « ى » shape in writing but doesn't change its pronunciation. This form of "a" always the final letter (never situated in the begining or middle of word).

Read

مَتى يَأتي موسىٰ مِنَ ٱلعَمَلِ
مُنىٰ تُراسِلْ سَلوىٰ

Vocabulary:

when   مَتى

he comes   يَأتي

she corresponds   تُراسِل

Chapter Twenty Four

ش　شـ　ـشـ　ـش

Like "sh" in sham

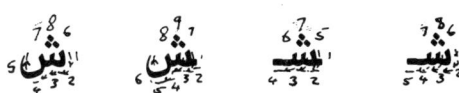

Pronouce the following syllables:

Like "sha" in sharp　شَا

Like she　شِي

Like "sha" in shade　شَّ

Like "sho" in shore　شُو

Read

شَامِلْ　وَلَدٌ نَشِيطٌ
إِشْتَرَى بَشِير　دَفْتَراً
نَامَ بَشِير بِالفِراشِ
شِمِّران　يَنقُشُ

Vocabulary:

active	نَشيط
he bought	إِشتَرَى
note book	دَفتَر
bed	فِراش
he is doing patterns	يَنقُش

Chapter Twenty Five

ذ

Like "th" in there (not as in thank), might be linked with the preceding letter, but must not be linked with the following one.

ذٰنِ

Read

طَلَبَ ٱلْأُسْتَاذُ مِن مُنذِرٍ أَن يَقْرَأَ ٱلدَّرسَ أَمامَ ٱلتلاميذِ

Vocabulary:

he asked	طَلَب
teacher, professor	أُستاذ
lesson	دَرس
in front	أَمام
students	تَلاميذ
student	تِلميذ

Chapter Twenty Six

ك ك ك ك

Like "c" in can

كِ لَكْ كِ كَ

Pronounce the following syllables:

Like "ca" in card   كا

Like « ke » in kept   كَ

Like key   كي

Read

كَريمٌ يَسكُنْ قريباً مِن بَيتِنا
سَأَلَ كَمالٌ مُبارَكَ؟
أَينَ لَقيت كِتابَك؟
قالَ مُبارك:
لَقيت كتابي فوقَ ٱلرَّفِ

Vocabulary:

he lives	يَسكن
near	قَريب
he asks	سَاَل
where	أَين
you found	لَقيت
your book	كِتابك
he said	قال
my book	كِتابي
on	فوق
shelf	رَّف
our home	بَيتَنا

Chapter Twenty Seven

هـ ـهـ ـه ه

Like "h" in hat

Pronounce the following syllables:

Like « ha » in hard   ها

Like « he » in help   هَـ

Read:

هادي° طالِبٌ
زارَني هاشِمٌ° يَومَ أَمسِ
قُلتُ لَهُ :
أَهلاً وَسَهلاً بِكَ
قابَلتُ والِدي قَبلَ سَفَرِهِ إلى فَرَنسا

Vocabulary:

He visited me	زارني
day	يَوم
yesterday	أَمس
I said	قُلت
welcome	أهلاً وسهلاً
I met	قابَلت
my father	والِدي
before	قَبل
his journey	سَفَرَه
France	فَرَنسا

Chapter Twenty Eight

ة   ـة

It is called taa **Kasserah** (short taa)

This "taa" dosen't differ in its pronunciation from taa taweelah « ت ». most feminine nouns end with taa kasserah (short taa), but are pronounced "h" " ه " when they are alone i.e

Plane طَائِره   Car سَيَّارهِ
School مَدْرَسه   Watch, hour ساعَه

But when they form words in a sentence (mostly) are changed into « ة ـة » "t" as below:

Read

السَّيارةُ قادمةٌ
رَكِبنا الطَّائِرةَ
فائِزةُ ذهَبت الى المدرسةِ مُبَكِرةً

Grammar:
If word ends with taa kasserah (ﺔً ةً)
which has (an //) the alif is not added
i.e.

مدرسةً   سيارةً

(see chapter seventeen)

Vocabulary:

(it or she) is coming	قادِمَه
we get on	رَكَبنا
she went	ذَهَبَت
early (for feminine)	مُبَكِرَه

Chapter Twenty Nine

ص ص‍ ‍ص‍ ‍ص

As a kind of "s" made with the blade of the tongue against the teeth ridge, the tip being behind the lower teeth

Read

ناصِرٌ يَصِلُ مُبَكِراً الى المَكتَبِ قَبلَ زُمَلائِهِ

صَبريَّةٌ تَقُصُّ القِماشَ بِالمِقَصِّ

Vocabulary:

he arrives	يَصِل
his colleagues	زُمَلائِه
she cut	تَقُصّ
cloth	قِماش
scissors	مِقَصّ

Chapter Thirty

ح ج جـ ـجـ ـج

It is pronounced as far back in the throat as possible, with the back of the tongue pressed down, as when the doctor presses it down with a spoon.

Read

حامِدٌ ۝ أطولُ مِن مَحمودٌ ۝
مَحاسِنٌ ۝ فَلّاحَةٌ تَقطِفُ ٱلأزهارَ مِنَ ٱلحَقلِ
صالِحٌ ۝ يَسبَحُ على شاطِيءِ ٱلبَحرِ

Vocabulary:

longer	أَطول
farmer	فَلّاحة
she picks	تَقطِف
flowers	أَزهار
farm	حَقل
he swims	يَسبَح
bank or shore	شاطِيء
sea	بَحر

Chapter Thirty One

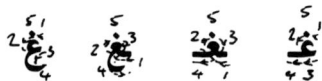

It is voiced back from the back of tongue towards soft palate

غُ غِ غَ غْ

Read

سُعادٌ وغَسّانٌ ذَهَبا الى اَلْغابةِ مَعَ فَريقٍ مِنَ الأَصدِقاءِ
اَلبِئرُ فارِغٌ مِنَ اَلْماءِ
يَصبَغُ مَحمودٌ غُرَفَ مَنزِلِهِ

Vocabulary:

they went (dual M.)	ذَهَبَا
Forest	غابة
group	فَريق
friends	أَصدِقاء
empty	فارِغ
he paints	يَصبَغ
rooms	غُرَف
his home	مَنزِلِه

Chapter Thirty Two

ضـ ضـ ض ض

It is made further back in the mouth with the tongue depressed in front and raised behind and as far from the teeth as possible.

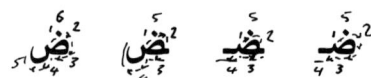

Read

ذَهَبَ أَحْمَدُ وغَالِبٌ الى حَوضِ السِباحَةِ

غُرَفُ البَيتِ ضَيقةٌ

سَلمى تَشْتَغِلُ مُضَيِّفَةً في إحدى شَرِكاتِ الطَّيرانِ

يَأكُلُ مُضَرُ في المَطعَمِ

Vocabulary:

he went	ذَهَبَ
pool	حَوض
swimming	سِباحة
small (for space)	ضَيقة
she works	تَشتَغِل
stewardess	مُضَيِفة
one of	إحدى
companies	شَرِكات
flight	طَيَران
he eats	يَأكُل
restaurant	مَطعم

Chapter Thirty Three

ج ـج ـجـ جـ

Like "j" in jam

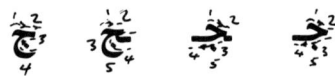

Read

جَميلٌ عادَ مِنَ ٱلسَّفَرِ
في وَسَطِ ٱلحَديقةِ شَجَرةٌ
يُعالِجُ ٱلطَّبيبُ ٱلمَريضَ
فَرَجٌ تِلميذٌ

Vocabulary :

journey	سَفَر
middle	وَسَط
garden	حَديقَة
tree	شَجَرة
he treats	يُعالِج
patient	مَريض

Chapter Thirty Four

ث   ثـ   ـثـ   ـث

Like "th" in thank (not as in than)

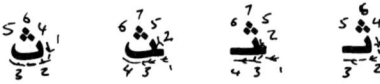

Read

ثَلاثَةُ كُتُبٍ على اَلرَّفِّ
يَحرُثُ اَلفَلّاحُ اَلأَرضَ
وَصَلنا في اَلسّاعةِ الثالِثةِ
أَفضَلُ اَلبِناءِ الحَديث

Vocabulary:

three	ثَلَاثَة
books	كُتُب
cultivate	يَحرُث
farmer (M)	فَلّاح
land (earth)	أَرض
we arrived	وَصَلنا
I prefer	أُفَضِّل
building	بِناء
modern	حَديث

Chapter Thirty Five

It is pronouced back of tongue towards soft palate, like ch in the scottish "loch" or German "ach", but more scrappy.

Read |

يَأخُذُ خالِدٌ ○ حَقيبَتِهِ
تَطبَخُ لَيلَى ○ اَلطَّعامَ
يَخرُجُ حامِدٌ ○ مِنَ ٱلبَيتِ متَوَجِّهاً الى مَحَطَةِ ٱلقِطار
حامِد طَبّاخٌ ماهِرٌ

Vocabulary:

he takes	يَأْخُذ
his bag	حَقيبته
she cooks	تَطبَخ
he goes out	يَخرج
towards	مُتَوَجِّهاً
station	مَحَطه
cook	طَبّاخ
skilled (adj.)	ماهِر

Chapter Thirty Six

ظ

It is made with the upper front of the tongue pressing against the bottom of the upper front teeth

Read

سَألَ مَحفوظٌ كاظِم :
عَلِمتُ أَنَكَ زُرتَ بَعضَ أَهوارِ ٱلعراقِ
كاظِم : نَعم لَقد زُرتَها وشاهَدتَ مَناظِرَها ٱلجَميلةَ

Vocabulary:

I knew	عَلِمت
you	أَنَك
visited (you or I)	زُرت
some	بَعض
marshes	أَهوار
yes	نَعم
yes I visited it	نَعَم لَقَد زُرتَها
I saw	شاهَدت
its views	مناظِرَها
beautiful (Feminine)	جَميله

Chapter Thirty Seven

Letters' names   أسماء الحروف

Letters names in order as they were mentioned before

ت : تاء	ا : ألف
س : سين	د : دال
ع : عين	ر : راء
ش : شين	و : واو
ذ : ذال	ن : نون
ك : كاف	ز : زاء
ه : هاء	ي : ياء
ص : صاد	ب : باء
ح : حاء	م : ميم
غ : غين	ق : قاف
ض : ضاء	ف : فاء
ج : جيم	ل : لام
ث : ثاء	ط : طاء
ظ : ظاد	خ : خاء

Chapter Thirty Eight

Sun and moon letters الحروف الشمسية والقمرية

letters are divided into two groups each has fourteen letters:

1) Sun letters:

ذ ، ر ، ن ، ز ، ل ، ط ، ت
س ، ش ، ذ ، ص ، ض ، ظ ، ث

when the above letters are preceded with a lif and Lam (الـ) Lam (ل) has not to be pronounced and the sun letter following it has to be strengthen by shaddah i.e.

اَلشَّمس ، اَلرَّبيع ، اَلنَّار ، اَلطَّائِر

2) Moon letters:

$$ ا ، و ، ي ، ب ، م ، ق ، ف $$
$$ ع ، ك ، ه ، ح ، غ ، خ ، ج $$

are pronounced as they are without
any change to haruf Lam (ل)
i.e.

$$ اَلعَمَل ، اَلكُرْسِّي ، اَلباب $$

Chapter Thirty Nine

"Hamza writing rules"
There is no strict rule governs Hamza writing, but we can say that most words with Hamzar are written with such rules have to be taken as guides.

1) Hamzah is connected with alif « ا » in the following cases:

a) if it is written in the begining of the word. i.e.

أَكتب ، أُريد ، أَتى ، إِنتَظِر

b) if it is preceded by haruf maftuh (a letter with fat-ha) i.e.

سَأَل ، يَأمُر ، نَقرَأ

2) it is written isolated:

a) when it was final and preceded by alif i.e.

ماء ، سَماء ، بِناء

b) if hamza in the middle and has fat-ha i.e.

جاءَت ، قِراءَة

3) Hamza is written on «ـئ»

a) if it is in the middle and has kasrah i.e.

يَئِن   قائِل   المدائِن   سُئِلٌ

b) if it is preceded by haruf maksur (a letter with kasrah) i.e.

بِئر   لِئام

4) it is written on wawoo (letter و) if it is preceded by haruf madmum (a letter with damah) i.e.

سُؤال   فُؤاد   سُؤدد

5) if hamza was final and preceded by haruf maksur (a letter with kasrah) it has to be written with haruf yaa (the letter   ) i.e.

قارِيء   دافِيء   ظامِيء

Chapter Forty

Arabic Numbers

Arabs invented the zero and the numbers which are used in Europe and other countries now, but later used the Indian numbers instead.

In the last few years some arab countries have returned to the use of their old numbers (which are used in Europe now).

Zero is pronounced صفر Sifr and written (٠) 'one' is pronounced Wahed واحد if it is Masculine and Wahedah واحدة if it is Feminine and written ١ and pronounced Ehdaa إحدا with attached pronoun i.e.

(one of them arrived) وصل إحداها

the following table shows the Arabic Numbers

		Masculine	Feminine
0	٠	صفر	صفر
1	١	واحد	واحدة
2	٢	اثنان	اثنتان
3	٣	ثلاثة	ثلاث
4	٤	أربعة	أربع
5	٥	خمسة	خمس
6	٦	ستة	ست
7	٧	سبعة	سبع
8	٨	ثمانية	ثمان
9	٩	تسعة	تسع
10	١٠	عشرة	عشر
11	١١	إحدى عشر	إحدى عشر
12	١٢	إثنا عشر	إثنتا عشر
13	١٣	ثلاثة عشر	ثلاث عشرة
14	١٤	أربع عشر	أربع عشرة
15	١٥	خمسة عشر	خمس عشرة
16	١٦	ستة عشر	ست عشرة
17	١٧	سبعة عشر	سبع عشرة
18	١٨	ثمانية عشر	ثماني عشرة
19	١٩	تسعة عشر	تسع عشرة
20	٢٠	عشرون	عشرون

For Masculine and Feminine

30	٣٠	ثلاثون	ثلاثون
40	٤٠	أربعون	أربعون
50	٥٠	خمسون	خمسون
60	٦٠	ستون	ستون
70	٧٠	سبعون	سبعون
80	٨٠	ثمانون	ثمانون
90	٩٠	تسعون	تسعون

All these numbers from 20 to 99 like those from 11—19 are followed by a noun in the accusative singular.

From upwards

100	١٠٠	مائة *	(1)
200	٢٠٠	مائتان (مئتان)	
300	٣٠٠	ثلاث مائة	(2)
400	٤٠٠	أربع مائة	
500	٥٠٠	خمس مائة	
600	٦٠٠	ست مائة	
700	٧٠٠	سبع مائة	
800	٨٠٠	ثمان مائة	
900	٩٠٠	تسع مائة	
1000	١٠٠٠	ألف	
2000	٢٠٠٠	ألفان	
3000	٣٠٠٠	ثلاثة آلاف	
etc. to 10000	١٠٠٠٠	عشرة آلاف	
11000	١١٠٠٠	أحد عشر ألفاً	
100,000	١٠٠٠٠٠	مائة ألف	
1000,000	١٠٠٠٠٠٠	مليون	

1 — 100 is written (مائة) but the alif is not pronounced
2 — Also is written (ثلاثمئة) or (ثلاثمائة)

Teach Yourself Arabic through a video cassette
(تعليم القراءة والكتابة العربية من خلال الفيديو)
Just watch and repeat.

The Film is the first one of its kind on the subject, and the Arabic on the Film is based on written and broadcast Arabic so it can be understood everywhere in the Arab world. It is designed to give a complete reading and writing Arabic course.

The Film lasts for two hours and thirty five minutes.

Methods Used in the Film
By displaying the Arabic letter showing each letter and how it is written and pronounced making syllables and words by combining letters, then displaying a passage at the end of each lesson and voicing these passages. The Film is divided into thirty six lessons and to give the student a special atmosphere the Film is made with an Arabic musical background and framed with Islamic and Arabic art.

Price: £25.00 or $36.00 per cassette (Beta, VHS or NTSC)
Plus £5.00 or $7.00 postage & packing by air mail or £2.00 in the U.K.
To obtain your copy please send cheque, postal order or international money order to:—

Distributed by
VOYAGE BOOKS
4 Carlisle Street,
London W1V 5RG
Tel: 01 434 2941.

Please indicate clearly which format you require.